Lingo Dingo
and the Romanian astronaut

Written by Mark Pallis
Illustrated by James Cottell

For my awesome sons - MP

For Sophia - JC

LINGO DINGO AND THE ROMANIAN ASTRONAUT

All rights reserved. This book or any portion thereof may not be reproduced or used in any manner whatsoever without the express written permission of the publisher except for the use of brief excerpts in a review.

Story edited by Natascha Biebow, Blue Elephant Storyshaping
First Printing, 2023
ISBN: 978-1-915337-79-5
Neu Westend Press

Lingo Dingo
and the Romanian astronaut

Written by Mark Pallis
Illustrated by James Cottell

NEU WESTEND
— PRESS —

This is Lingo. She's a Dingo and she loves helping.
Anyone. Anytime. Anyhow.

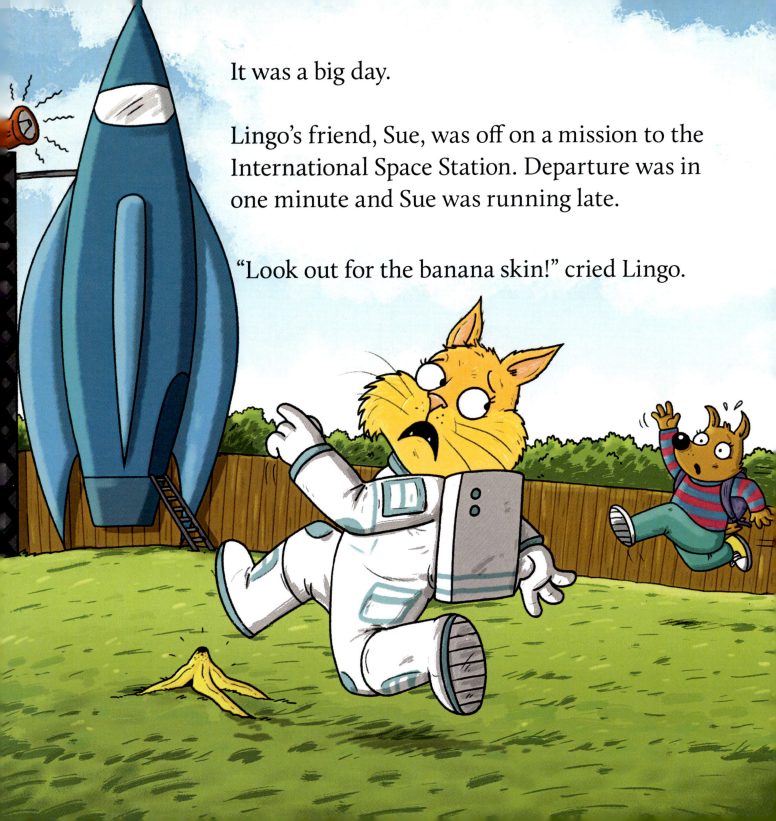

It was a big day.

Lingo's friend, Sue, was off on a mission to the International Space Station. Departure was in one minute and Sue was running late.

"Look out for the banana skin!" cried Lingo.

"I'll be OK, but the mission is over," said Sue.

"I can help!" said Lingo.

But there were only thirty seconds to launch: hurry Lingo!

Quick as a shooting star, Lingo climbed up into the rocket.

"Don't forget this. It's a battery for the Space Station," said Sue.

The countdown began: Five, four...

Lingo soon arrived at the International Space Station.

She was in space and she could f l o a t !

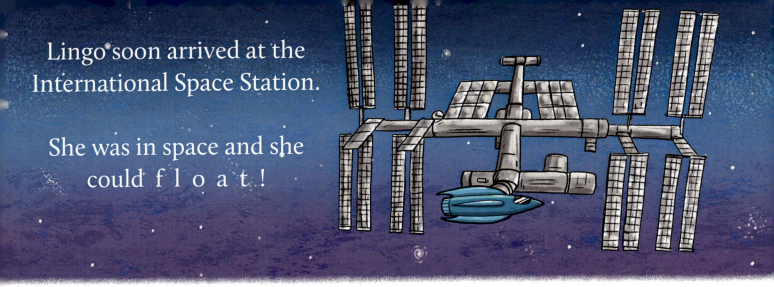

"Bine ai venit," said an astronaut. "Numele meu este Rex. Sunt astronaut." Lingo tried a reply in Romanian, "Numele meu este Lingo."

Bine ai venit = Welcome; **Numele meu este** = My name is; **Sunt astronaut** = I am an astronaut

"Vino," said Rex. He led Lingo around the Space station. "Toaleta."

"Laboratorul."

"Dormitorul. Și ursulețul meu de pluș."

vino = come; Toaleta = the toilet; Laboratorul = the laboratory
Dormitorul = the bedroom; Și ursulețul meu de pluș = and my teddybear

Suddenly a BEEPING blared out!
"Ai bateria nouă?" asked Rex.
Lingo wasn't sure what 'bateria' meant. She checked her pockets!

Ai bateria nouă? = have you got the new battery?
bateria = battery; **nouă** = new

"Întoarce-l la stânga," said Rex, pointing to the handle.

Lingo turned it right. "Nu dreapta, stânga!" cried Rex. Lingo turned it left and the hatch swung open.

dreapta = right; **stânga** = left
Nu dreapta, stânga! = not right, left; **Întoarce-l la stânga** = turn it to the left

Space was waiting for them!
They got straight to work changing the battery.
"Dă-mi șurubelnița, te rog," said Rex.

Lingo passed Rex the screwdriver and he screwed the new battery into place.

șurubelnița = screwdriver; **Dă-mi șurubelnița, te rog** = pass me the screwdriver please

"Succes! Bate palma," he said.

Lingo realised Rex wanted a high five.

Success!

Lingo called Sue with the good news:

Succes = success; **bate palma** = high five

The view was incredible.

Rex pointed out all the things to see.

"Soarele."

"Pământul."

Pământul = earth; **Soarele** = the sun

Stelele = the stars; **luna** = the moon; **Brațul robotic** = robotic arm

"Ursulețul meu de pluș!" cried Rex.
Rex's teddy must have floated out of the airlock.
"Folosește brațul robotic," he said.

Lingo was going to use the robotic arm.

Ursulețul meu de pluș! = my teddy; **Folosește brațul robotic** = use the robotic arm

Her fishing rod! Lingo swung the hook

Pumnii strânși = fingers crossed

- "Pumnii strânși," said Rex - and caught Teddy's bow tie!

"Prietenul meu," cheered Rex. "Să sărbătorim."

Prietenul meu = my friend; **Să sărbătorim** = let's celebrate

Rex pressed a button and funky music boomed out.

Time to bust some zero gravity dance moves.

"Eu dansez, tu dansezi, ursulețul de pluș dansează, noi dansăm," laughed Rex.

Eu dansez = I dance; **tu dansezi** = you dance;
ursulețul de pluș dansează = teddy dances; **noi dansăm** = we dance

"Zâmbește," said Rex, and took a photo.

Zâmbește = say cheese

"Îți este sete?" asked Rex. He squeezed big blobs of water over to Lingo. "Este apă," he said. "Îți este foame?" asked Rex.

Îți este sete? = are you thirsty?; **Este apă** = this is water; **Îți este foame?** = are you hungry?

Lingo and Rex snuggled into bed. What an incredible day.

"Îmi place spațiul cosmic," said Rex.
"Da," agreed Lingo.
"Somn ușor, Lingo," said Rex.

Îmi place spațiul cosmic = I love space

Lingo didn't have time to wonder what 'somn uşor' meant, she was already fast asleep.

Somn uşor = sleep well

Learning to love languages

An additional language opens a child's mind, broadens their horizons and enriches their emotional life. Research has shown that the time between a child's birth and their sixth or seventh birthday is a "golden period" when they are most receptive to new languages. This is because they have an in-built ability to distinguish the sounds they hear and make sense of them. The Story-powered Language Learning Method taps into these natural abilities.

How the story-powered language learning method works

We create an emotionally engaging and funny story for children and adults to enjoy together, just like any other picture book. Studies show that social interaction, like enjoying a book together, is critical in language learning.

Through the story, we introduce a relatable character who speaks only in the new language. This helps build empathy and a positive attitude towards people who speak different languages. These are both important aspects in laying the foundations for lasting language acquisition in a child's life.

As the story progresses, the child naturally works with the characters to discover the meanings of a wide range of fun new words. Strategic use of humour ensures that this subconscious learning is rewarded with laughter; the child feels good and the first seeds of a lifelong love of languages are sown.

For more information, and books in OVER 50 different languages visit www.markpallis.com

You can learn more words and phrases with these hilarious, heartwarming stories from **NEU WESTEND PRESS**

Available in over 50 different languages!

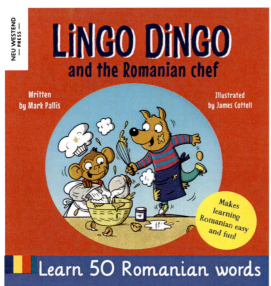
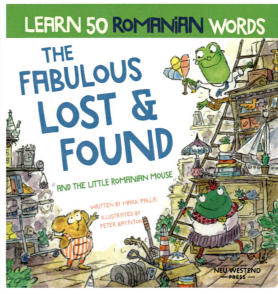

@MARK_PALLIS on twitter
www.markpallis.com

To download your FREE certifcate, and more cool stuff, visit
www.MarkPallis.com

@jamescottell on INSTAGRAM
www.jamescottellstudios.co.uk

"I want people to be so busy laughing, they don't realise they're learning!"
Mark Pallis

Crab and Whale is the bestselling story of how a little Crab helps a big Whale. It's carefully designed to help even the most energetic children find a moment of calm and focus. It also includes a special mindful breathing exercise and affirmation for children.

Featured as one of Mindful.org's 'Seven Mindful Children's books'

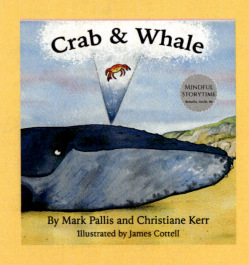

Do you call them hugs or cuddles?

In this funny, heartwarming story, you will laugh out loud as two loveable gibbons try to figure out if a hug is better than a cuddle and, in the process, learn how to get along.

A perfect story for anyone who loves a hug (or a cuddle!)

www.markpallis.com

Manufactured by Amazon.ca
Acheson, AB